ODES

The Sign of Saturn: Poems 1980–87
The Father
The Wellspring
Blood, Tin, Straw
The Unswept Room
Selected Poems
One Secret Thing
Stag's Leap

ODES

Sharon Olds

CAPE POETRY

1 3 5 7 9 10 8 6 4 2

Jonathan Cape, an imprint of Vintage,
20 Vauxhall Bridge Road,
London SW1V 2SA

Jonathan Cape is part of the Penguin Random House
group of companies whose addresses can be found at
global.penguinrandomhouse.com

 Penguin
Random House
UK

First published by Jonathan Cape in 2016

penguin.co.uk/vintage

A CIP catalogue record for this book is available
from the British Library

ISBN 9781911214069

Typeset in India by Thomson Digital Pvt Ltd, Noida, Delhi

Printed and bound in Great Britain by T. J. International Ltd, Padstow, Cornwall

Penguin Random House is committed to a sustainable future for
our business, our readers and our planet. This book is made
from Forest Stewardship Council® certified paper.

MIX
Paper from
responsible sources
FSC
www.fsc.org   FSC® C018179

for Carl

CONTENTS

7

ODES

ODE TO THE HYMEN

I don't know when you came into being,
inside me, when I was inside my mother –
maybe when the involuntary
muscles were setting, like rose jello.
I love to think of you then, so whole, so
impervious, you and the clitoris as
safe as the lives in which you were housed, they would have
had to kill both my mother and me
to get at either of you. I love her, at this
moment, as the big fortress around me, the
matronhead around the sweetmeat
of my maidenhead. I don't know who
invented you – to keep a girl's inwards
clean and well-cupboarded. Dear wall,
dear gate, dear stile, dear Dutch door, not a
cat-flap nor a swinging door
but a one-time piñata. How many places in the
body were made to be destroyed
once? You were very sturdy, weren't you,
you took your job seriously – I'd never
felt such pain – you were the hourglass lady
the magician saws in two. I was proud of you,
turning to a cupful of the bright arterial
ingredient. And how lucky we were,
you and I, that we got to choose
when, and with whom, and where, and why – plush
pincushion, somehow related
to statues that wept. It happened on the rug
of a borrowed living room, but I felt
as if we were in Diana's woods –
he, and I, and you, together,
or as if we were where the magma from the core of the
earth burst up through the floor of the sea.

3

Thank you for your life and death,
thank you for your flower-girl walk
before me, throwing down your scarlet
petals. It would be years before
I married – years before I carried, within me,
a tiny, baby hymen, near the
eggs with other teentsy hymens
within them – but you unscrolled the carpet,
leading me into the animal life
of a woman. You were a sort of blood
mother to me: first you held me
close, for eighteen years, and then
you let me go.

I

ODE TO THE CLITORIS

Little eagerness;
flower-girl basket of soft thorn
and petal, near the entry of the satin
column of the inner aisle;
scout in the wilderness; wild ear
which perks up; tender dowser, which points;
imp; shape-shifter; bench-pressing biceps of a
teeny goddess who is buff; lotus
for grief; weentsy Minerva who springs
full-armored, molten – I did not know you,
at seven, I thought you were God's way
of addressing me, when I kept swinging
on the rings, after the bell had rung . . .
He didn't use his words, he used
you to get my attention, he wrenched me
and wrenched me, then, in six or seven
wrenches of my body and brain, you
the living wrench which winched the wrenches.
Later, you would do that without God –
with boys, with kisses, and later you'd become
an instrument of love's music. Today,
I saw your portrait for the first time, your
dorsal vein, your artery, your
cavernous body, your vestibular bulb,
your suspensory ligament – and I
could see how evolution got
the idea from you, to invent an organ
something like you but a lot bigger.
You were named for a Greek hill, *klinein,*
a slope – you are the ground of our being, the tiny
figure of the human, the hooded stranger who
comes to the door, and if we bless her we will be blessed.

ODE TO THE PENIS

Someone told me that what I write
about men is objectifying. So I ask you,
O general idea of the penis, do you mind
being noticed? You who stand, in the mind –
erect and not, old and young –
for all your representations, O abstract
principle, haven't you maybe been
waiting for your turn to be praised? I think
you're lovely and brave, and so interesting, you are
like a creature, with your head, and trunk,
as if you have a life of your own. But you are
innocent, you are not your own man,
you are no more responsible for your actions
than the matter of the brain for its thoughts. And you've had
    a mixed
history – you've been taken into
carnage, as the instrument
of it, and you yourself have been played
to produce the desperate screams. Often
you have not been protected, nor used to protect,
and oft not been respected, nor wielded
to respect. And yet most of your history
has been spent in joy. And I wonder how it
has felt, being so adored as you have been,
and feared. And what is it like, for you – if you could
look down, from your Platonic cloud
of categories – when two of you
are engaged together, or married – yourself
primed, yourself to your own power?
And being a concept, are you smart, do you know
you're equal to your sister concept,
and even that you came from her,
back at the invention of the separate male –

the ovaries heavying down toward the earth,
the organ of orgasm growing and growing.
I cannot imagine you, from within – but as a
sage said of a god, I do not want
to be sugar, I want to taste sugar!
But that's just my heteromania talking,
and you're not homo or hetero – or visible
or manifest, you do not exist
except as an imaginary quorum
of all your instances. So I'm not
flirting with you, I'm just saying
I like you – not as an object but
a subject, a prime mover, a working
theory of plumbing and ecstasy,
a boy's pride and anxiety,
wind sock of zephyr and gale, half
of the equation of creation.

ODE OF BROKEN LOYALTY

I want to go back to that day, when it
was broken in me, the loyalty
to family, when I was cut free,
or cut myself free, from the fully human,
and floated off, like an astronaut
untethered. I want to go back to the hour
some cord in my mind was cut, and I no longer
was fed by the placenta of the nuclear
or extended family, but aborted
myself or was aborted from that house. Once torn
away, once shunned and shunning, it seemed there was
little I could not write about, I felt
as if my disenfranchisement
had been undone, I was out on the wind, like a
spinster alone in orgasm,
like a witch, but I thought I was thinking and trilling
for everyone, in every land
and time. I was insane. Was I insane? I thought
that someone driven out beyond the silence
of normal reticence could speak
for the normal. I don't want to go back
to the hour I broke and ran, the broken
yolk and albumen shining in the toothed
bowls of the shell. I like to say
it might have been I who broke the contract,
as if it were not obvious
it was broken, physically, in me.
I want to go back to when I found the paper,
and the ink, as if the matter of the planet
wanted to chant, and be chanted, as if one could
think oneself loyal, being loyal to that chant.

WIND ODE

I saw the water, ruffled like a duck,
as if its ruffles arose from within.
I saw clouds, scudding across
as if by their own will. I sat here,
over the pond, and saw its fierce
gooseflesh and its rough chop
as if it were shivering. I did not know you,
I looked right through you. And then, one summer
day, Wild Goose was in nine moods
at once, and I went down to it,
and into it up to my lower eyelids, and I
saw a row of fine lines
rushing toward me, then another row
cross-hatching it, rushing, then a veil of dots swift
in, like a hat-veil-sized spirit, I saw you,
it was you, and there were many of you, I sank
underwater, and looked up,
and saw your strokes indent the surface.
Could we trace them back, these hachures and gravures,
to the Coriolis force caused by the
spinning of the earth? Who is the mother
of the wind, who is its father? O ancestor,
O child of heat and cold, wild
original scribbler!

ODE TO MY WHITENESS

after Evie Shockley

You were invisible to me.
You went without saying.
You were my weapon secret from myself.
Whatever I got, you helped get it for me.
You were my ignorance.
Because of you I was not innocent.
I did not see that – you were my blinding light.
My dreams had a blank area in the center,
taking up most of the screen they played on in my sleep –
a blazing circle that blanked out the core of the scene.
I thought it was my mother's violence,
but it was you, too.
You the unseen fat which fed me in the wilderness.
You my masonic handshake.
You my stealth.
You my drone.
You my collaborator.
You my magician's cloak of steam,
you my dissembler.
You, mine? I, yours,
irisless eyeball, you my blindness,
inspiration of my helpless act,
you my silence. Evie's blackness
a dancer, you another, the two of you moving together.

AMARYLLIS ODE

When the blossoms were wilting, I cut the stalk
and put it in a glass, before my trip – to have
waiting, for me, the damp withering
blooms to see, when I came back.
I thought of the female side of my gene-
alogy – the mothers, who have liked to have
waiting, upstairs, a daughter stripped
to be punished, and I realised I had been my mother's
conduit to the satisfaction
of being, in her own time,
the beater. I think she did not know what she was
doing. And it *is* nice, isn't it,
to have something waiting, the knowledge of which
will thrill you – how much drier will the blossoms
be, how everted each pistil-tip on its
coral stalk dusted with ochre
seed? My mother and I were a twosome, as her
mother and she had been, and her mother's
mother ... Mine used to perform a tune –
not while she was beating on me –
White coral bells, upon a silver stalk. It was
a pleasure, for me, to behead-head-head-head
the amaryllis, to slit its throat.
The last verse was O *don't you wish*
that you could hear them ring?
That will happen only when
the fairies sing – or in our case,
when the dead mothers weep – my mother would weep,
  to read this.

ODE TO MY SISTER

I know why they say the heart is in
the heart. When you think about people you love,
you get warm, there. I want to thank
my sister for loving me, which taught me
to love. I'm not sure what she loved in me,
besides my love for her – maybe
that I was a copy of her, half-size –
then three-quarters, then size. In the snapshots, you see her
keeping an eye on me, I was a little wild,
and I said silly things, and she would laugh her serious
laugh. My sister knew things,
sometimes she knew everything,
as if she'd been born knowing. And I
so did not know – my wonder went
along with me wherever we'd go,
as if I had it on a tool belt –
I understood almost nothing, and I
loved *pertinding,* and I loved to go into the
garden and dance with the flowers, which danced
with me without hardly moving their green
legs, I was like a music box
dropped on my head. And I was bad –
but I don't think my sister thought I was actually
bad, I was her somewhat smaller
littermate – nor did she need
my badness to establish her goodness. And she
was beautiful, with a moral beauty, she would
glide by, in the hall, like a queen
on a barge on the Nile, she had straight black hair
that moved like a black waterfall, as
one thing, like a black silk skirt.
She was the human. I aspired to her.
And she stood   between   the god   and me.

And her hair (*pertind*) was like a wing
of night, and in my dream she could hold it
over me, and hide me. Of course,
by day, if the god wanted you for something,
she took you. I think if the god had known how to
take my curly hair from my head,
she would have. And I think there was nothing my sister
wanted to take from me. Why would
she want to, she had everything –
in our room she had control of the door,
closed, or open, and the light switch,
dark, or bright. And if anything
had happened to me, I think my sister
would not have known who she was, I was almost
as essential to her, as she to me.
If anything had happened to her,
I think I would not be alive today,
and no one would remember me,
as if I had not lived.

2

ODE TO THE CONDOM

Rubber; safe; French letter; sleeve;
protector of the young so young
they do not yet exist; separator
of male and female; bundling board down the
middle of a Shaker bed; mechitza
down the aisle of an Orthodox synagogue;
veil between the matters which create
spirits; Trojan; trumpet mute;
latex; superfine; reservoir tip;
Ramses, Fourex – some actually
made of sheep intestine, sparkling
with mammalian life – I never liked you.
Of course I'd hardly recognise
you now, what with your flavors, your Ribbed
for Her, your cap and bells, but bless you:
separator of women and men
from abortion; separator of health
from death; separator of male
from male, of well from ill – costume of the
life force, best friend of the earth.

ODE TO THE TAMPON

Inside-out clothing;
queen's robe;
white-jacketed worker who clears the table
prepared for the feast which goes uneaten;
hospital orderly; straitjacket
which takes, into its folded wings,
the spirit of the uncapturable one;
soldier's coat;
dry dock for the boat not taken;
seeker of the red light of stars
which have ceased to be before we see them;
bloodhound;
unhonored one; undertaker;
secret-keeper;
you who in the cross-section diagram,
before the eyes of a girl child,
glide into potential space,
out of the second-stage rocket's cardboard cylinder,
up beyond the atmosphere,
where no one has gone before;
you who began life as a seed in topsoil,
you who blossomed into the air like steam from a whale's
    blow-hole,
you who were compressed into a dense calyx,
nib which dips into a forty-year river;
mute calligrapher – we write you here.

HIP REPLACEMENT ODE

A week later, when it takes me only
a couple of minutes to get out of bed,
when I can sit up, in the living room
with my partner, and watch the Knicks win,
when I'm well enough that he can go home
to the trees, the pond, the winter garden
of the sky, I suddenly get it that the head of my
femur is gone, I could never find it again,
even if I could go through the hospital garbage –
and I miss it, I mourn it, knob of a cane
which helped me go wherever I went,
shepherd's crook I leaned on and moved forward,
and danced, lovely ridiculous motion, like
a game, a toy, a wild spurt of happy will,
like the sexual play the newel post of the
acetabulum was quiet
household witness to – the bone
made by my father and mother, inside
my mother, or made by nature's arts
and crafts, inside her, like a stem, a green
shoot in the womb, which would grow to a branch, a sore
bole, I had had no doubt I wanted it
out, replaced by a joint like a plastic and
titanium one-legged cricket, but this morning
I wanted to reach back, for it, through the
swabs in the waste can of the surgical theater,
assemble the jigsaw and piece it together, like
seeking back through a lifetime to find
the grains of love – the grains of reasonable function.

ODE WITH A SILENCE IN IT

Pink sky in the morning—a girl's sky.
Slowly the trees become visible,
and the spaces between them. Imagine being
able to walk, into the woods,
without fear. If my classmate had not
been taken, and –

        leave a silence here –

and murdered, and buried in the woods near our houses,
would I be as afraid? Rape is rape
which alters where it alteration finds,
and bends with the remover to remove. 'Legitimate
rape,' the politician said – rape born to rape's
legal parents. Parent rape,
family rape, date rape,
gang rape, priest and rabbi
rape, coach rape, rape of
eighty-year-olds, eight-year-olds,
eight-month-olds, morning rape,
noon rape, night rape,
spring rape, summer rape,
fall rape, winter rape,
Army rape, Navy rape,
red sky in the morning,
Air Force rape, Marines rape,
world rape – how many, each minute –
the end of the world rape, the first
rape. Do all primates rape? Is all ape
sex between consenting apes?
Do dogs rape? Do spiders rape?
Sex between the parts of a flower
has such tenderness, the honeybee

dusting the dost-thou-take from anther
to pistil. Where else but with us, the policy
of rape, of rape pregnancy,
and rape birth. What is the sweetest
word? Is *consent* the sweetest word
on earth? It has a *con* in it, a
girl's own spiral universe.

ODE TO THE LAST THIRTY-EIGHT
TREES IN NEW YORK CITY
VISIBLE FROM THIS WINDOW

A thousand windows look down on them.
One crown looks like a granite mountain
peeling in layers, a thousand breaths
a day. One looks, from above, like a bomb,
an exploded shell, a thousand petals.
One is a thriving colony of green
ants milling, a thousand workers,
one like a swarm of pupae, writhing,
one like chartreuse firecrackers with a
sharp Chinese ideogram
on each fragment, a thousand words,
and one is like a thousand paper cranes,
emerald and yellow. Hundreds of years ago,
here, ash were used to make
a bitter sugar, later to make
baseball bats, and across the Pacific
the U.S. printed human bodies,
as ashes, into sidewalks. Honey locust
thorns were used for pins and spear points,
black locust for fence posts – and snowshoe
hare, and mourning dove, ate
the seeds. Oaks gave acorns, to eat,
and to fatten pigs with – 'laws provided
that anyone wantonly injuring or destroying
an oak should be fined according to the size of the
tree and its ability to bear fruits.'
Mostly what the trees do, now,
is breathe with us, give us natural
artificial respiration.
All will be cut at the waist, the branches
will go with the usual legs and arms into the wood chipper.

The elm, which once fed partridge and opossum,
is getting out on its own, while it can,
it will not stay to witness the killing,
it died the week the judge ruled.
Several rulers live in sight
of these ancient beings, and one of them,
who sees this grove, every day, has the
power to prevent the pyre, to enforce
his guardianship of this arbor, this land,
and air, and water, and green fire.

ODE TO MY LIVING FRIENDS

(January, 2010)

What a lengthy gap there has been between deaths!
It seems as if none of those closest to us
has gone, for what seems months. For me,
it's been so long that when I think of someone
dying, I think of my mother and father,
my ferryers in out of nothing, out of the
temporary rich something they were made of.
I have carried them with me – not like a partial
twin, in a sling in front of and against me,
but in my body, in my brain cells. But you,
my friends, my chosen and chosen-by ones,
I see you as built-in aspects of the earth,
like elements, like members of the periodic
table. I know, we're mortal – the open
door is there. But for weeks and weeks I have
forgotten that I'm going to lose
every one of you, until
the ones who are left lose me. When I
was a child, I could not have lost you, I did not
know that I would find you! – I'm blessed that it
will happen to me. Before it does,
let me say: you were exactly who I'd been
looking for, without daring to imagine.
Breast that presses against other breasts it was you!
Root of wash'd sweet-flag! timorous pond-snipe! nest of guarded
duplicate eggs! It was you!
Hands I have taken, face I have kiss'd, mortal I have ever
touch'd, it was you.

ODE OF WITHERED CLEAVAGE

When I saw it for the first time,
I was baffled that anyone would walk out her door
showing that – the vines, the snakes,
the ripples, the nest of nestlings' necks!
And to think that on an ancestor
of that – if withered cleavage is
a descendant of fresh, young breasts –
I had spent some early hours of my life,
learning to adore the curves of the creamy
moon. My mother's desire to be touched,
late in her life, was so intense I could
almost hear it, like a keening from the hundred little
purselets of each nipple, each like a
rose-red eraser come alive and starvacious.
And now my own declivity is
arroyoing, and if I live long enough
my chest over my breastbone may look like
an internal organ, a heart trailing its
arteries and veins. I want to praise
what goes one way, what never recovers.
I want to live to an age when I look
hardly human, I want to love them
equally, birth and its daughter and
mother, death.

3

ODE TO MENSTRUAL BLOOD

I do not know if you are dead or alive, rich
sloughed rations; tube of space-flight
nourishment discarded; offal – what falls
away, what is made from scratch near where love
is made. You are a boy's blanket,
and a girl's blanket, you are male and female –
servant; magician; mother; father;
god of the possible – departing, mostly,
unneeded, you who in our ignorance
have been despised. We have feared the pieces
in you, the proteins and monocytes,
and sugars, and macrophagocytes, and bi-
valent iron atoms, as if they could be
pieces of us. Stream by whose banks
we doze and kiss, thank you for our hope of
survival which you are alert to as any
first responder. Go down in honor, through the
pipes and treatment plants and rivers,
to the sea, and be drawn up, from it, into
clouds, and in your altered form
rain down upon your people, hardy
elixir, transparent manna.

CELIBATE'S ODE TO BALLS

When I first saw a naked man,
there they were, visible,
in air, in light, hidden in
their carrying case, inside them the tiny
people, teeming seeds of them,
the world populations, the crowds
rushing across enormous capital–
city squares, as if a man
could feel his known world tilt
and the oceans lift up out of their beds.
And when I was no longer married,
once I was a spinster again,
every day I missed living with them
– with him, but the longer I went without him,
the more the longing was general, cate-
gorical, and imperative.
I missed the two who are with the one
which enters, while they do not enter,
they loll intense,
I missed how they are two in one –
once, in a dream, I wandered in one,
my oldest home, my hobo-sack home,
I underwater-breaststroked through
the dessert of it, like the inside
of a tongue, and light came through into the pink
male sewing reticule,
basket of tangles of brilliant polished
thread – and then the skin would shift
like my scalp when the hairs stood straight on end.
All those years, when I was celibate again,
I'd cry out to balls, 'O purses of X's
and Y's, O inside-out pocket with its dear

seam, O dear,' I knew that some
would laugh when I said it, 'I love balls,'
and others would groan with me a moment, missing them.

ODE TO THOUGHT

I can almost see you, in the air – like a species
in your own right. I'd thought you were something
I made, when I was in my room,
alone with my scissors, Scotch tape, and paper –
and you were there, doing god-knows-what
while I cut, moving my jawbones in tune
with the blades. Were you using your words, or playing with your
   alphabets, or less fettered than that, just
scooting your protons and neutrons and electrons
around. I know – you were something between
an electric current and a wave, in grey
and white brain-flesh. O thought, you were
inside me, but it didn't seem so,
I thought of you in a skirt of dazzle,
flying. You darling, you're beyond comprehension,
you travel in and out of our heads
at your own whim, and we are innocent
of all you say – and there's no blood on your hands,
dear thought, though I've killed so many of your kind there's been
a lot of your blood on mine – no more, go
roam, fill the room, go out
upon the earth, go to and fro,
and up and down, in it, I know you will
come back: see how my eyes get wet when I say it, *I am sane.*

SECONDARY BOYCOTT ODE

I had never seen anything like it. I was walking
out of the office of the braces doctor,
in the same building as the acne doctor,
I was on my way to the lunch counter
that had sandwiches on soft bread
with the crusts cut off – & people were blocking
the doors, following each other around
in a circle, like our junior high marching band,
& they were in the way, between me
& my sandwich. I went up to a lady who was watching,
& asked her what was happening,
& she told me about the segregated
lunch counters in the South – this was
a secondary boycott, of Woolworth's. & I asked,
how do they choose who walks, & she said,
Anyone can. I had never seen anyone
saying no with their body, with their feet.
When I stepped toward the circle, a man walked a little
faster, & a woman walked a little slower,
& there was a space for me, to sing
without making a sound, at last to be
unfaithful to my family,
stepping out on silence.

LEGS ODE

After they opened my flank up,
and chopped down the femur, and into its marrow-hole
drove the shank of the metal joint,
and closed the book of my flesh, and sewed it
shut, they said, Don't cross your legs, you could
dislocate the new hip –
and if you do, you will know it, that leg will be
four or five inches longer
than the other, and the pain will make childbirth seem
like nothing. So, for six months,
I did not make that first braid
of the caduceus, I gave up the deployment,
the flash of the seated entrechat, I
did not throw one leg over
the other leg's line, in thrilling enjambement.
I had not known how vain I was
of my gams, until I had to still them – no
semaphoric waving, no
Rockette Rockette-flanked. But at last
I could not resist, and like a happy sadist
uncoiling her lustrous bullwhip, and flicking it
out, I unleashed my tensile weapons,
again, as if their length was a gift
of additional mortal time. And as the live
dough of my loaves, my raw baguettes, rolled
out and snapped back, as my fish leapt and
dove into the water again, as my trained
Lipizzaners curvetted, I felt like
someone whom a regime has not
allowed to pray now folding her hands,
fervent unfolding and folding. What
is self-esteem? The last time
my mother beat me, she could not beat me,

because she could not catch me – I ran
from her, and when she cornered me, I
looked down, and saw the top
of her head, as if the prayers of all those
years had been answered, I'd been lifted up,
and up, above her, on the stilts of my new
adolescent legs, I would never
wrap them around her waist again
and my arms around her sides, sobbing
to be taken back, when she'd broken my spirit once
more, pulled its pestle out of the
mortar of my life. *Whooosh!* I whirl
my living sword, she can never go back to that eden.

UNMATCHING LEGS ODE

I don't know why I am fairly cheerful
about my unmatching legs. I am not
cheerful about my foot soles, which were
like two brains, reading the ground,
and now have less than half their nerves, they are the
numbskulls to whom I trust my balance, their
surfaces crinkled tinfoil rubber.
But when I lie on the floor, on my back,
and look up, at my lower limbs, those
tapered feelers, I like them, even
though you cannot tell if the left is
withered or the right fat – the right
is swollen. When I was a new matron,
I thought that the blue-green line down my inner
calf – the great saphenous vein –
was a Nile beauty mark, and the way it
rose, when I was carrying my first young, there was
something cool in how it fit between the
ledges of the gastrocnemius
and soleus, like a snake between two
strata of rock. So when I see the leg's mass,
I am almost proud of it, that it could
fit in it one and a half of its fellow.
And the skinny leg, the original one,
how can it be that I like the healed
gouge on it, from the edge of the porch
stair, when I fell upwards, or the one
from the corner fang of the truck door,
they hold the places I've been, they are like
passport stamps from his kingdom. I have always
liked my legs, the double stem
which lifts the big odd flower of me up
and up. It's as if I fell in love

with them, when they and I began
to learn to walk together. The two of them were
best friends, who could press against each other
and feel the love, at the top of the stalks, and they were
twins – not identical, but
mirror twins, loving the other was
loving the self, they were ecstatics, they were
the thyrsus and the stylus, the healthy narcissus.
I'm sad they will rot. I wish our bodies
could leave us when they are done with us –
leave our spirits here, and walk away.

MATCHING ODE

She must be 70, now – I hope
she is still alive, not yet in the ground, not yet
taking in topsoil and giving it out
as a hominid earthworm. And if she is alive,
the pretty hair of her lower body
is sparsening, though not yet back
to the slight down we both were growing,
that summer, age 12, spinsters of the parish,
readers of movie magazines.
I don't know whose idea it was,
probably mine, for one of us
to strike a bathing-beauty pose,
in the dark, in our shortie nighties, and say Now,
and the other would turn the flashlight on,
and run it over the Girl Scout imaginary glamour.
Thrilling to lower a shoulder strap, to
smolder. And those scant, cotton froufrous,
they never came all the way off, I think that
would have seemed dirty, and what we were doing
was secret and intensely sweet. And we were
matching, the skinny bodies and elongate
legs and the little new puddles of the breasts with that
small drupe on top – we were a matched
set, which lay outside society,
outside reproduction, in our own
culture of early flashes of sexual
insight. And when we ceased our play,
and hugged goodnight, before sleep, she supine, I
prone on her – of course, a top –
what happened, in that sharp little organ, that
soft beak, between my legs,
was like the joke buzzer the boys
would have in their palm and shake your hand,

but bigger than that, more like the time-lapse
hibiscus full-blossoming, fast-motion, in pulses, in the school movie.
It happened for a summer – or for a week
of summer. We were from different schools,
and neighborhoods, and we parted, but together we'd been
radiant, amoral first-timers at the passion of the mortal.

ODE OF GIRLS' THINGS

I loved the things that were ours – pink gloves,
hankies with a pastoral scene in one corner.
There was a lot we were not allowed to do,
but what we were allowed to do was ours,
dolls you carry by the leg, and dolls'
clothes you would put on, or take off –
someone who was *yours,* who did not
have the rights of her own nakedness,
and who had a smooth body, with its
untouchable place, which you would never touch, even on her,
    you had been cured of that.
And some of the dolls had hard-rubber hands, with
dimples, and though you were not supposed to, you could
bite off the ends of the fingers when you could not stand it.
And though you'd never be allowed to, say, drive a bus,
or do anything that had to be done right, there was a
teeny carton, in you, of eggs
so minute they were invisible.
And there would be milk, in you, too – real
milk! And you could wear a skirt, you could
be a bellflower – up under its
cone the complex shape like a closed
buckle, intricate groove and tongue,
where something like God's power over you lived.
And it turned out you shared some things with boys –
the alphabet was not just theirs –
and you could make forays over into their territory,
you could have what you could have because it was yours,
and a little of what was theirs, because
you took it. Much later, you'd have to give things
up, too, to make it fair – long

42

hair, skirts, even breasts, a pair
of raspberry-colored pumps which a friend
wanted to put on, if they would fit his foot, and they did.

4

BLOW JOB ODE

I never thought of it as a line
of work. I did not think of myself with my
lunch pail going to my profession and punching
the time clock in and out. Surely
that practice was not divided into
management – who were owners – and staff,
who had no share in the profit. Job?
Is that what they thought, that it was boring for us
and we couldn't wait till we could break for lunch?
They thought they were rulers, commanding us
against our will? It's weird thinking about it
from a boss's point of view, looking down
at the working head, the alienated
labor – looking down the pay scale. But. If we
were both engaged in the same act
it wouldn't be employment, would it, but play,
play in the house of the gods of pleasure.
At least *blow* is not a word from commerce,
but the golden rule of music: know
as you would be known, blow as you would be blown.

ODE TO THE FEMALE REPRODUCTIVE
SYSTEM

I first saw you in a simple line
drawing, black and white, on an unfolded
sheet of insertion instructions, the side
view of a girl – a passageway, at a
slant, up and back, to a blunt,
humble thing, like the outline
of a wading bird's bowed head
made on a wall by a drooped hand
held in the beam of a flashlight in the dark.
Later I saw you in an illustration
in a magazine, in full, damsel
color, the middle sister between
the magenta genie of the rectum and the little
stork dancer of the urinary bladder
up on the fine, slender leg
of the ureter. All three of you
had a rosy enclosedness, but you
were the central grace. And when I saw you, in a textbook
of anatomy, full frontal, I saw
a feral unseeing creature, like a she-ram
with great fallopian horns. In some drawings,
the fimbrial fringe at the frayed end of the
tube was reaching out, with a beckoning
suction, toward the ovary, as if
sirening up an egg – and in others
the entire apparatus of you
looked like a ghost costume, the child in it
making the haunted *Woooo, woooo*.
But mostly it looked like an instrument, a
graceful lyre, which would be played in me
to call a being forth from another
world, from the future, bringing her own harp with her.

SEXIST ODE

On the way to Bethlehem, when it was
time to nurse my stuffed bear,
I pulled up my undershirt with confidence, I
too would have breasts, like the cartons with spouts
school milk came in – open the roof
and pour. I believed I would get to have babies
and nurse them, and when my chest, like a mushroom
darkroom, began to push up its domes,
I felt I had them coming to me. And one
decade more, when the cream came in, and the
sugar loaves became rock candy, it was
scary, but it had been promised to me.
I have heard a small boy declare
he is pregnant, then glance into a grown-up's eye
to see if it might be true. Soon enough, the boys
would call each other by the fighting words, *you
girl, you cunning wussycat, you
puss.* But I got to make mud pies,
and cut out paper clothes with tabs,
and put on pink satin hooves
and clomp in the rosin box. I knew we seemed less
powerful, but I felt like one of the
truly human. It would make me queasy
to become a fleshly cake, and queasier
a living cake box, but even though
the boys had got off easy, I felt I had
got off easier.

SPOON ODE

Spoon of O, spoon of nothing,
spoon of ankh, spoon of *poonss,*
spoon of the lady at the dressing table,
spoon of ♀, spoon of female,
spoon of ♂, spoon of war,
spoon of the world, spoon of War of the
Worlds, spoon of stick figure,
spoon of � girl, spoon of ♗ boy,
spoon of ⟶⟍⟋ spear thrower, spoon of fire,
spoon of egg, spoon of egg race,
spoon of dish, spoon of ran away with,
spoon of ran away with and came back, spoon of never came back,
spoon of silver, spoon of gold,
spoon of milk, spoon of Saturn,
spoon of vulva, spoon of vagina,
spoon of Ant, spoon of Bee,
spoon of Venus, spoon of Serena,
spoon of vugg, spoon of vum,
spoon of spider, spoon of sun,
spoon of fee, fie, foe, fum.
Spoon of everyone. Spoon
of the belly. Spoon of the empty belly.
Spoon of the full one. Spoon of no one
hungry. Spoon for everyone.

ODE TO BUTTERMILK

You were neither of my favorite foods —
you were the two together, two rights
making a wrong. Everything else
was a liquid or a solid, but you had pieces
in you, which passed the bare nerve of the
uvula and gave it a flick,
like that eighth-grade boy, in the hall, passing
the new nipple of a seventh-grade girl.
And what *was* that, in you? Chopped-up babies?
Trying to hold you down, almost force-
fed in the restaurant, I became
a buttermilk martyr, the hero of a True Blue
Cafeteria booth drama.
If a child gagged, a child tried again,
until its face and shirt were like
the center of a circle jerk.
Except for you, there was nothing I'd be offered
I would not eat — I would not be offered
eyeballs, but your bits and clots were like
the brains boys put your hand in, in the dark, on
Halloween, the warm spaghetti
to bring out your natural scream. Today,
I understood you were innocent, you'd been
taken from a nurser and her nursling, then churned
until you turned. You were landscape — the place,
the means, the stream on which a father could float
his frat-boy hazing. Dear milk, dear butter,
have fun together — matter benevolent
before your corruption by the sapiens spirit.
Enjoy your clotted nature, pallid
rapids, maybe you're like a girl

with ova in her which are related to her father,
or maybe you're like my father's daughter's
love of him with the tart treats of hate in it.

ODE OF THE CORNER I WAS STOOD IN

They did not have time-outs then, they had
Go stand in the corner. And though your back was to
the room, so a younger brother could come in,
unseen, but heard, and could caper, and gloat –
maenad sisters and brothers!, so many
children who were not onlies had companion
furies roughly their own size! –
if you were standing in the corner, for some reason there would
be no bend-over to God that day.
So you stood, in geometry solitary,
staring at the right angle
until it would pulse a little – isosceles,
acute, isosceles, acute, and you could
even stare hard enough so you were
up against an inner silo
wall, in at the curved edge of your
own diorama, not
a wood rat or an oviraptor but a
living-room feral child. And you could lean and
caress your face in the cheekbone protractor
declivity of your burrow, like practicing
nose-rub kisses with your sister. You were bad,
you might be facing a hard, empty
life, but you were making friends
with architecture, a science of shelter,
and maybe practising for the future,
for dying, when you'd face the finite
end of your own universe,
maybe no fire, no brimstone, no fork
of pitch, if you were lucky – and standing in the corner,
fully clothed, upright, you *felt* lucky.

ODE TO THE CREATURE FROM THE BLACK LAGOON

I'm not sure how old I was,
not still twelve, I think, that child
lifted up on her telescoping legs –
and not yet fourteen, that worst year,
trying to talk to the other kids
through the agency of the monster I shuffled
around as – I think thirteen, I think
it was sometime during that thirteen-month
night, that I snuck out to see it. It was not
human, though it had a torso and limbs
and a head, and it did seem a little like us
in its isolation and suffering
and menace. Mostly it shined, mostly
it glistened, its craquelure skin mirroring
light, mostly I think it hunted
people, mostly it came up,
out of the Black Lagoon, and wandered
a town, one of its kind – an it, post-
human and yet pre-alien.
It pains me now to think of the actor
in the glitter suit – no penis, as far as I
could see, though I had not seen one yet – no
breasts, I who was growing my own small
butter lettuces in the night, or
being used to grow them. O bifurcate
sparkling with costume scales, O primate –
from the planet inside us – your thin skin
the gliss flay of the juices my possessed
body was making, thank you for showing us
ourselves, shimmering up out of

the night soup of the gene, thank you for your
beauty, your invincible strangeness, your dangerous
stardom, your fearlessness, your slime!

5

DOUCHE-BAG ODE

When I hear the young refer to someone as a
douche bag, I want to say, You may have
never *seen* a douche bag. They were red
rubber bags, like hot water bottles, you'd
fill it and hang it high enough
so that gravity ... I can't go on,
I see my mother's douche bag, my poor
douche-bag mom's pathetic douche bag with its
clamps, and its aorta tubes,
dangling over the bathtub, awesomely
shameful, and which reminded me
I'd been some kind of catsup Halloween
costume in her, almost before I was
bipedal. And so to call someone a
saline sac – let's take some pity
on the creepiness of how women were treated
in the 1950s. It drove my mother
crazy, but she did the best she could –
she never turned and said, I could have got
rid of you, my little valentine,
but I gave you the warm, rose-colored lunch bag
of the placenta: I gave you my heart, to eat.
And now I remember it, not my mother's
but mine, like a dowry – lock the door, then
hang it from the shower rod like food hung over
a bough, out of animal reach,
slide the perforated wand inside you then un-
clasp the clamp, and Lo!, you are
a night clearing, in which a fountain
of Aphrodite leaps up, and cascades
down, making her notes, her brine
sea chanty, her sparkling douche-bag song.

SINGLE LADY'S ODE

And then, when I have been single for years,
bell with a phantom clapper, I wonder
how I took in – how I gave my
mouth and throat over to almost
the whole thing. I remember relaxing, as if
reminding myself no harm would come, and then
fitting my alveolar valve, like a
cape, around the glans's shoulders – as if
clothing, in softness, that part of the man
in the part of me which was the part of music
and speech, as if he were a song I was pouring
forth by taking in. I don't
remember how I breathed, but I breathed.
And my fortune was such that I did nothing with a man
which I did not want to do. If I'd been more
adventurous, I could have done things
with men I did not love, who did not
love me, but I did not want to,
it seemed too extreme a trust to give,
so I've done it with hardly anyone, done it
a lot with hardly anyone.
Well, I have lost my taste for my ex,
over these years since he left, he seems
covered with her now, covered with her,
so what I miss the most, about
that act I had never heard of, or imagined – which I
thought the first man who gave me
the chance at it had that moment invented –
is not a specific person, but a man-in-
general's familiar which could take its strong flight
along my inner swallow-way ...

I miss not the representative
of its kind, I miss the man I have
in mind, the brain and soul behind
the organ that comes inside, the man
I have not met yet.

ODE TO WHISKERS

Rumi said it – the price of a kiss
is your life. After divorce, I felt
that my passion for dots, for dominoes,
and ocelots, and ladybugs,
and dotted Swiss's spots – for deckle,
for scattered speckle – was part and parcel of the
love of shaved whiskers, the blasphemous worship
of whiskers. They presented concepts of addition,
and square roots, and multiplication,
and the coefficient, they presented the fact
of desire, they presented a formula for it:
rasp over skin times caress to the power of the
burn. There was almost nothing I liked
better on earth than those beds of passion's
nails – the ease with which they're grown,
as if it was simple to be a man,
as if it felt as glorious to them
to be it, as for us to be pressed to it –
beauty of what one is, beauty
of what one is not. Sometimes he had lain his
cheek to mine so slow the iron
gentleman spikes, excitement-bright,
would sink into my skin, as if entryways
were ready in it to receive them. The direct
communication between that male
jaw and this female knee joint – the needles
which turned the pins to water – seemed planned by
advocates of reproduction
berserk with advocacy. Which is to
say, I think some saints have kneeled in their
caves, longing for their god, much as I
craved the return of five o'clock shadow.
Sometimes I could hardly believe

how long I might have to last with that craving.
Sometimes I regretted that I could not dally, but I
tried it once, when I was a fresh left
wife, to go with a man who was not into
love, it nearly killed me, my heart
is my body, the price of a kiss is your life.

SPLIT ODE

for   *Chase Twichell*

Thinking of you   this morning, the day
after your operation,   it is
as if you are in   two places
at once –   the first place is you,
and the second place   is where what had been
in you lies,   what they lifted out,
and set aside.   In my sleep I saw it
on a gurney,   womb and fallopian tubes
like the ceremonial   mask of a deer
or like a violet lyre,   being rushed
to where our entrails   are read. The chrome
tray flashed under   the ceiling lights,
in it both   chamois purses,
full at your birth,   now spent – and attached
to each of them   something like a waxing
predator moon.   I woke, and sank back, and you were
lying on a desk,   like a fancy deckled
scalloped stationery   envelope,
and a letter was being   pulled out,
and put back and pulled out   like those tabs in children's
pop-up books,   and the letter said *isthmus,
infundibulum,   fimbria.*
And then, you were a map,   of a pale
golden color,   and something like
the Louisiana Purchase,   of a blue-
violet color,   was in you, and then gone –
first in you, then   drifted home, to another
continent.   I turned onto my back,
and my ventral surface   was a dress pattern
and the dotted lines   were stitches made
of flame. And at first   light I dreamed you were
spirit;   and what had been removed from you

64

was matter.   And at dawn, in your hospital bed, there was
a big deck   of 53
cards, and the doctors   slipped one out –
an extra, red   queen, and then there were
many, little   decks on the sheet
around the mother   deck – maybe 30
decks of 52   weeks each,
and all of them had   a yin and yang
on the back of them,   every woman
jack of them.

ODE OF THE PRESENT MOMENT,
IN THE LIVING ROOM, WITH BIANCA

The weaker roses in the nosegay are sagging down onto the
    stronger ones.
One of them is collapsed into an oval,
as if there were labia monumental and labia generosa
and labia major and labia soubrette and labia minor.
Under the violent clouds of the bouquet,
the picture on the table, Red Satan, with wings like black oak
    leaves,
with eland horns. The man we saw in the park
had a curtain of flies around him, like a corpse,
flies of lusciousness, flies of circumstance,
dipterae of soot pulling Satan's pocket chariots,
moving evil through the world,
person to person. I knew no evil,
I saw no evil, I heard no evil,
just some minor wickedness, some
sickness, which I caught. And have contained it,
mostly, as a Venus's trap contains and digests.
There was never a metal witch which flew through the air –
there was that beaten nearly to death face
which came down toward my bed in the night from the corner
    of the ceiling.
It was not a man, it was not a woman.
It was one of my familiars. I think it had something
to do with looking up from within the full bathtub,
my head at the level of my mother's knees,
looking up and seeing her bearded possession
with its little tidbits and extras and tails hanging out,
and a drop of bush-liquid in which my face
was miniature and upside-down.
Part of the beauty of male genitals, to me,
was that they were not anything like my mother's.

Nor are mine like my mother's – as long as I do not see them.
Birthday cakes, with their spiral piping,
and their sugar roses, have looked to me like what my
there felt like, my between-my-legs
which was officially not good, but was secretly everything. On
the table,
a pair of socks with very alert owls on them.
And suddenly a noise of extreme legal danger,
and past the window, low over the river, go
six fighter jets in a triangle, as if
announcing, with joy, at last, total world war.
Then they are gone, their noise of things being crushed and
ground up is gone,
only their ash-brown contrails remain,
and slowly break up, into a burned fur,
the remains in the taxidermist's window of the last original
creature.

STANLEY KUNITZ ODE

Ninety-five years before he died,
Stanley found an abandoned kitten
in the woods of Worcester. Stanley's father
had drunk Drano in a public park, while
Stanley had still been turning, a nebula
slowly taking kunitziform
inside his mother. And when he found
the lost cat, he took it home
and gave it a box in the attic, under
the stars where his father was wheeling, and he raised
his feline companion – I don't know girl
or boy – without his mother much noticing,
hard as she worked, silent as she kept.
And his pet grew, and when they got to the woods he would
take off the collar and leash and they would
frolic together, she-he/he-she would
teach Stanley, already sinuous,
to slink and hunt. And I don't know who it
was who suddenly saw that Stanley's
companion, growing stronger and bigger and
lither, was a bobcat, and none of us
was there the night Stanley released her-him
or there when it rose in him, the desire
to seek a feline of his own species.
And when he was ninety-eight, and Elise
had gone ahead, leaving her words and
images behind her, casting the skin of them,
I saw, in a city in Ohio, an elegant
shaving-brush-soft replica bobcat,
and brought it back to West 12th, along with the
usual chocolates, and flowers, and a demo of my
latest progress toward a model's sashay on the catwalk.
And after that, when I'd come over,

Stanley would be holding the stuffed
animal, and petting it,
nape to rump, nape to rump,
stub of the bob tail – 98,
99, 100, those huge old elegant
hands, stroking the world, which hummed when Stanley stroked it.

SHEFFIELD MOUNTAIN ODE

for Galway Kinnell

And then, in the morning, the stillness of the quiet
skirts of the dark, on the ground, around
the full-moon trees, four a.m. –
I can feel the moon *moving,* actually
circling us, as we seem to circle
the sun, as we rotate toward it, the Sheffield
mountain like the corolla of a flower
turning toward our birth star. Before I leave,
I go into his room, where there is the being
suffering. '*Oh!* – it's still
da-ark,' I say, with the falling cadence of
surprise on *dark.* '*Ye*-es,' he says,
on the same notes, like a rhyme with the meter.
Then he groans, prone on the bed, holding to the
covers, holding to the turning earth,
and he sleeps. It is just past the Days of Awe –
the New Year, and Yom Kippur,
days and evening at temple with my partner –
'I hope you have an easy fast,'
I whisper to my friend, who is never again,
soon, to eat the food of this life which is the
only food we will have. 'Thank you
for being my best friend,' and my voice
warbles like the first bird of the morning.
Oom pompa *noo* suc – you fish your side
of the river, I'll fish mine, you said
it meant – and I can see us, decades,
fishing both sides of the river,
together, sharing the catch. Safe
travels, I say to the shape in the hospice
bed, the metal of which catches light to make
a constellation. Then I'm going past a plowed

field, water in the valleys of the harrow's
talons, on the water the upside-down
crowns of bare trees, mist above the creek
rising like fine baby hair, I am
driving as the crow flies,
beside the crow.

SAN FRANCISCO BAY DAWN ODE

When I have come down, from thousands of feet
up, in the mountains, down to sea level,
to the shore of my birth, it is clear to me
that I would have protected my mother from her mother
if I could have. But it was so hard to get at her,
that grandmother, from where I was,
still deep inside my child mother.
I had, as yet, no arms, or legs,
or head, no power to heal my mother's
mother. If I had existed,
if I had had the wings of the morning,
I would have taken that large, turbulent
cold one on. I would have walked in,
when she was in a room alone,
my mother's mother,
and spoken to her. But I was Knoxed up
so tight, in her daughter. I wish I could have
sung, to that daughter, my mother, from within her,
sung to the crux and rip of her ravage
in her own mother's house,
I want to be able to go back there – though
as yet without the breath of the earth,
or a mouth, though missing half of myself – to
release into my mom's young life
some whole notes, some spirit-level
bubbles, mercury burps of psalm
to rise within her, and gently break open
in her throat. There. Now I can sink back
down into the sleep of the clutch
in her side, down in the reeds, where the local
feathered heads and necks are pulling
from underneath the wading-bird wings,
and in the pocks of the tidal mud

the brine is rising, now, and light
is touching it, from thousands of feet,
thousands of miles in the air.

SICK COUCH ODE

As long as I am motionless there is a humming in my arms and legs
    that feels as if I am healing.
But when I lift the field guide to look at the Sierras,
the book is so heavy with all the granite in it
the urn of my upper torso starts to indicate that it will slosh soon,
it is like a lyre being played by golden infected water,
aeolian harp played by big insects of mucus.
When I lie still, they gradually stop playing.
Then the life in me is simple and primary,
a breath like a kindergarten block, A,
another, B, I would like to be quick and cute,
but even when I'm well I'm slow, slow and alert,
now I am not too alert, I am resting,
gradations of the *i*'s in *virii*,
I am sitting way low on the couch, the back of my
head leaning on the upholstery curve,
I forget why I decided I am brutal but I decided it,
now I am an Anglo-Saxon broadsword, of the bendable kind,
laid down, my feet out far away on the seat of a chair.
A tiredness like a potion in my arms,
I try to love my neck but it seems unlovable.
I think I am brutal because I come from brutal people.
I blow my nose, and out of the holes in the
back shoot pieces like green popcorn,
I am a sick brute – this is sickness talking.
Wellness says It's all right, sickness, we understand you need attention.
I am writing without moving my arm or eyes
and it's exhausting me. I don't take death seriously.
I thought it was brave to work until you got seriously ill – low
    notes, lower . . .
In my dreams there is no kindness – toward me or by me.

But now I am awake, I breathe deep – no slur from the lungs!
Now I am matter, and I'm going to be kind to it.
Ah sleep in daytime blackness. Sweet dreams, rumpled broadsword.

6

VICTUALS DREAM ODE

Inside my father's testicle, tonight, it seems
brilliant and satiny, valentinaceous,
as if I had come from his heart, and was
a part of him. And as soon as he gave me
up – fierce kiss goodbye –
I traveled into the mystery
of the half-human journeying toward the half-
human, into the chamber, the vault
in the murk, and then his matter bumped
her matter and they createred my spirit. He seemed
not to mind that I was partly my mother,
I think it was a kick, to him,
himself as a girl, sired off a lady.
That is why I like to believe
I was conceived in my father, carried in that rosy
hammock, I felt he disliked me so much
less than she did, he did not uncare for
his eyes in me, or his oddball mind,
or his lanky legs – or her bones in me,
her cheeks and chin, her eyelids. All those dinners she cooked,
eaten in the silence he decreed. Peas
were interesting, the way they were rebels
in a group. Gravy could drown whole families.
And then there was chewing, big relief, and thank
god for meat, for what we regarded as the
lower creatures, and their vitals, liver
and lights, brains, eggs, balls and heart.

ODE TO THE WORD *VULVA*

Dear word, I feel for you – as a baby
feels for hers, as her arm is getting long enough –
that you're on the page with *vulgar,* and *Vulgate
Latin.* But there is *vowel,* as well, and
vugg, Cornish for a hollow in a lode,
crystal-lined. And I like the source
of your name, **wel-,* to turn, roll,
roll up, wrap, you are like a set of
crepes (from Latin for curly or wavy),
or a folded carton – not take-away
but keep. There is lots of official language
in your definition—like a court case –
*external, genital, female, mammal,
majora, minora,* but we know you are the mounds
and glides which safekeep the singing key
to the soar up into another world –
from which an almost born one might
descend, a being who often wears you, for some
moments, as a rolled lapel,
the last word in the fashion of the living
costume, as the child is emerging through
the double trapdoor in from the future.
Vulva! I love ya two *v*'s, ya
mouth within a mouth, I love ya
music we make, saying you, with our
teeth and lower lip and tongue,
I love that you come from our planet which is made of
atoms of star stuff, like the Milky Way,
like the constellation Vulpecula –
the fox, between the Dolphin and the Northern Cross.

TOXIC SHOCK ODE

Her church still felt like the hull of a homemade
redwood boat. Over the altar,
Jesus was still wearing blue, his heavy
thigh thrust forward in the swirl of his skirt.
When I got to the hospital, they were changing
the dressing – they'd stripped her pus-filled vein
and barely saved her life. My mother
was lying like a child witch on the bed,
her silver hair streaming back from her miniature
face. I held her hand as they bared
the seven holes where they'd eased the swollen
vein free. She lay there,
looking at me, while the doctor squirted
water into each slit, and pulled
a foot of crumpled gauze out of each, she
shrieked a little, baring her gums and
teeth in an agonised, girlish look, then he
took the syringe, and irrigated
the pits again. She glanced and then looked
at my face in a furtive way, and said,
Not very pretty. I stroked her hair – poor
beautiful woman. I patted her awhile,
she mourned her sleeveless evening dresses
one by one, by house, by place
of purchase, and saleslady, and first night worn, her
attendants of Eros, then she dozed, and I gazed at her,
ark that brought me here, as if rescuing me from matter.

ODE TO WATTLES

I want to write about my wattles – oooo, I
lust after it,
I want to hold a mirror under my
chin so I can see the new
events in solid geometry
occurring below my jaw, which was
all bone till now, and now is jam-packed
reticule. I love to be a little
disgusting, to go as far as I can
into the thrilling unloveliness
of an elderwoman's aging. It is like daring
time, and the ancient laws of eros,
at once. But when I look down,
into the compact's pool, and see
my face hanging down from the bottom of my face,
like a raft woven of popsicle sticks,
my nursing-home neck,
then, though I'm willing to age and die
for there to be sex and children,
the slackness of the drapery, and the
inside-out pockets of the jowls shock me.
I thought it wouldn't go so far with me
that I would be geology,
my throat a rippling of synclines and anticlines
back when the crust was warm, and I
was hot. Secretly, I don't know yet
that I'm not, but I bow my head to time,
and count my withered chins, three five seven
nine, my muses, my truth which is not
beauty – my crone beauty, in its first youth.

REAL ESTATE ODE

If the Pyramid at Giza were at
Bleecker and La Guardia,
the base would extend down to West Broadway
and Spring, and across Spring to Mercer,
and up Mercer to Bleecker and across
Bleecker to La Guardia,
sloping up on four sides
to its peak the height of the skyscraper
on Spring and Varick. It would be
the home of one
person, one
dead person, and of others made dead
to keep him company, in his deadness –
and the home of a GNP of plunder
mined from the earth and from the lives of the miners,
and it would be solid, except for the chamber
of the hoarder, and it would weigh thirteen billion
two hundred twenty-four million
pounds. A Pharaoh, a University
President, an Executive Officer
Chief could slip his trousers under-
neath it at night, and they would come out very
flat in the morning, with a killer crease.

ODE TO MY FAT

Palpating my arthritic joint –
my saddlebag feels like a treasure ball,
dime-store treats wound in crepe-paper
streamer, so that they bulge with rubber
babies, with balls and jacks, yet I feel
it isn't dishonorable to wear
these pockets of flesh like the quilted pouches
of ladies' lingerie bags. And there are calf-skin
Florentine boxes made with multi-humped
lids like this, and Elizabethan
sleeves made of bunches of puffs.
And somewhere there is a fish roe which is
a ball of bubbles, and a rhizome,
or a diatom, in the form of a sphere
made of half-spheres, and probably there's
a teething toy. And how about
a mathematical formula, which
describes a dome covered with domes,
or a cabochon-cut gem then cut with
baby cabochonettes. I know, it's
unnerving – they're collapsible and
bounce-backable, apop and aquiver as a
spider egg-mass, the blobulettes
of fat, fecund as Astarte with her chest
of a hundred breasts – it's papadodeca-
hedral as the blastocoele
itself, it's like a doppelgänger of what
each of us started as – exponentiating
matter. Yet I salute you, elderly
corsage, wilted hydrangea worn
at the hip, holster of life force,

fat of wonder, fat of bright
survival, O tapioca, O foam
of Aphrodite, O cellulite!

MY MOTHER'S FLASHLIGHT ODE

Sitting in the early morning dark,
holding her junior-size chrome flashlight.
In the cylinder, the batteries shift
and roll, like two, double A,
winged monkey bombs. I write by
her light. When she had gone into her final coma,
and I was on the jet to her,
flying toward her as if I was
a locust swarm, powering my way through the
air with my laugh, my *I'll get you Dorothy,*
it mattered to me beyond intensely
that I get there before she died, that I hold her
alive, knowing it would end, knowing
she was not, after all, infinite.
I don't think my mother knew what she meant
to me, I don't think I knew. At night, when she was
elderly, she would flash me, poor
lonely soul, I would sense the slow
pink-white meteor of her unclothed body
begin to approach me from deep in her room.
I wanted to run, there was something hard to
take about it, I'd steer her and turn her,
as if I was wearing her own, old,
pliable, terry-cloth oven mitts
to carry something too hot to touch
to a family table. My mother flashed me.
I write by her beam. My mother shone
with will, she traveled across the low
sky above my crib caroling, I sing
by her song, at dawn she is my lantern, I sing by her light.

ODE TO STRETCH MARKS

I thought you were just in the epidermis –
the thinnest outer layer of us,
like wind on water – now I learn you go
down through the dermis, you fill its fissures,
and down further, through Malpighi's layer,
and the connective tissue, even the sub-
cutaneous cellular area,
maybe a Meissner's or Ruffini's or Krause's
corpuscle torn in two when you parted
the seas of the epithelium.
When the heart leaps up, do you appear in the epi-
cardium? And do you arrive,
like good spirits, to attend a boy's first
erections? Do you gather, over nine months, in the
endometrium, the mucous
tunic of the uterus?
The way you gleamed, I knew you must be
scar tissue, but I did not know what you
were for. Now I think you're like a warning label –
a faint scrawling on the hips and breasts
of someone who has carried and nursed: this vehicle
has been driven, this vessel has contained, it is not
as far as it is possible to be
from its use-by date. I always thought
you were exquisite, the way you caught
the light, like the figures woven into cloth
made on a loom by Monsieur Jacquard –
the gleaming ripples in the silk. But then
I always liked old ladies, I had never
met one who looked as if she wanted

to beat me up. So the language of aging,
the code of it, the etching, and the scribbling
and silvering, are signs, to me, of
getting to live out my full term,
enduring to become what I have loved.

MERKIN ODE

(merkin, n. a pubic wig)

When I first heard the word *merkin,* I thought it had
something to do with mermaids and mermen, all
fresh fish below the waist.
And when I learned what a merkin was –
a little wig for the nether pate,
a fake beard for the nether face –
I wondered why anyone would want one. But now,
in the shower, when I look down, I see
the shapely, dense riot of gleaming
coils is beginning to be quelled, my shrub
is in retreat, its wilderness
a little pushed back – my weeds are being,
by time, gently whacked. And in the order
in which they arrived, so are they, in reverse,
leaving, drawing back from their
heraldic border, withdrawing like ladies
to the withdrawing room, until someday they will be –
if I am lucky, and get to grow old –
like an adolescent boy's mustache
around the lips. When the first wisp
appeared, I would gaze down, as if it was a
thread of smoke from a fire at a great
distance, and when the second and third
arrived together, I thought of them as
party ribbons, streamers for a maypole's
reverse space up into my ground,
and in a dream they were whisker faerie
soldiers sprung up to guard an inward
candy mountain. And now the earth
provides, on my body, more and more signs:
No Fishing, No Eggs, Out of Milk. And as I am
heading, with a nice slowness, for the state of non-

being – instead of mourning loss,
or pasting, on Venus, a hirsute mask, I would
praise the waning alphabet
of nests and crescents and springs and spirals,
the pelf of having had, at both ends,
curly hair, like matter hugging itself.

WILD ODE

Early summer morning, the sun just up.
I was thinking about women's farts,
and men's farts. Whether or not
a woman's fart is legally hers,
is it female? And there, above my table,
outside the window, was a barn spider,
walking, drawing a line of shining
out of its rear end – the pursed
lips of its spinneret pulsating.
And I wondered who the web legally
belongs to. The arias my mother warbled –
are there traces of them, still, in the sky,
delicate waves, on which a speck of her
dust could sit, like a half note
on the bar of a musical score? And are her farts
there, somewhere, might one be perched
near a fart of my father's? The air is not female
or male, or it's both, and it's all the other genders –
one individual gender
for each of us. Have I gone as far as I can
go, on these lines I pull out of my ass?
Women smoked cigarettes,
with the delicate circular lip of their sex.
They did not do this for the sight of other
women nor did women pay them to do it.
Nor was this done only in the past
tense. I think they blow smoke rings. I think
we are insane, and sane. There are people in every
town, and state, and country, begging,
at this moment, for mercy.

7

ODE FOR THE VAGINA

Sitting on the clothlet (*toilet* comes from a
diminutive for *cloth*), I was reading an empty
Rx box, and it had the word
vaginal, in ten places, in
bright red, and before I recycled, I was
tearing all the *vaginal*s
into rough pieces, *ina, va,*
gin, and then I noticed what I was
doing – that poor clean word, I was
ashamed of it. I liked the way
my partner said it, he simply said it –
from talking about breeding, the cows
approaching estrus – but the rest of us seem to
pause before we say it, as if the word
is dangerous. It might be disgusting that I
want to bring poetry into the bathroom,
like a pal, a buddy in fear-time, a tune
when you're scared. There is so much pain, in bathrooms,
sometimes enough to make me pray
or weep, and then there is all the blood and the
not blood, all the not
motherhood and the motherhood,
and now I understand I need not
apologise, I can say *vagina*
and look you in the eye, even though
she was named after the penis, after its
need for her – from the Latin, *vagina,*
'scabbard, sheath'.

ODE TO THE GLANS

I know – why did I wait until now,
the last moment, almost the moment
after the last moment, to sing
to you, outermost, tender, heart.
Respect held me back, and shyness.
Before I first saw you, I had not
seen even a picture of you, and you were
fearsome – when it would come down to it,
between you and my maidenhead,
I knew I could trust you to push until I was
torn from my virginity –
and you were adorable, you and the penis
like the dearest most basic doll, you were like
a brain without a skull, you were like
a soul. When I was eye to eye,
for the first time, with you, and I saw you
weep, the gleaming tear emerge
from the top of your mind, from your fontanelle,
I saw how it was going to be – it was
going to be what the movie in the theater of the
blossoming flower had promised, the rich
spongy corolla, the firm male
softness, it was going to be
mercy, and ecstasy – and, in there,
there were real babies, tiny, brand-new,
with tinier babies inside them, enough
to last a lifetime, and beyond a lifetime and a lifetime.

SECOND ODE TO THE HYMEN

My partner says that what I write
about women is self-involved – 'You're sixty
something years old,' he exclaims, 'and still
writing about the first time you got laid!'
But it isn't just *my* hymen –
people get to talk about Beauty and Truth,
why not address, directly, the human
maidenhead, the Platonic form
of her, the putting off intercourse until
the girl will not be torn apart by full-term birth,
why not lament the hymen being hunted
and plundered, impaled on a pike in a public
square like a tiny severed head.
Isn't it time to praise the crimson
music she makes, once, the small
death which marks the beginning of an inner
life, and the species continuing?
O clenched fist which opens, O knot
which is cut, O spherical trapdoor which is
pressed, pressed, and gives way, ripping,
I'm calling up a hymn for your honoring,
looking toward the day, as if it could come,
when your disposition will be left to the great
city of the girl which stands all around you.
Many things have been called sacred
to the many religions founded on earth –
oh if we could declare you sovereign
over yourself, little night blood sister,
picnic basket of pain and free will,
bright civil right!

ODE TO A COMPOSTING TOILET

And then, at the nature retreat, there
it was, the magic chamber – in goes
one thing, out comes another – where what
we make is made into fertilizer,
the hopper an enamel tank, where the liquids
are separated from the solids, where the enzymes do
their labor, and what can be used again
sinks down to where it can be harvested,
near-odorless. We do not think
our shit smells good, but we do not think
the globe should be turned into a great cesspool
to accommodate our desire to part from our
offal as fast as possible.
In this drying cabinet, shit happens,
and then, over time, it alters its nature,
its million busy toxins die,
it turns to arable waste – waste
no longer, waste not want not. As in
a blood bank, but dirtier,
soilier, the effluvium of the offspring
of the planet mingles: fertilizer of
New Hampshire, Kenya, New York, Boston –
Yankees shit, Red Sox shit,
in excremental harmony;
Vegan shit, kosher shit,
slow food, fast, vegetarian,
fruititarian, even the sorrowful
wisps of anorexic shit,
and Calvinist shit, and Kabbala shit,
Halliburton employee shit,
Orthodox shit, Puritan shit,
Lesbian shit, nympho virgin
poet chick shit. Seas and rivers

love the composting toilet, lakes and
streams sparkle its praises, and the small
creatures of the pond and creek
keen for it — dark green machine
like a porcelain throne, its royal flush
inside it. Come sit on it, come be
its queen, or king.

ODE TO DIRT

Dear dirt, I am sorry I slighted you,
I thought that you were only the background
for the leading characters – the plants
and animals and human animals.
It's as if I had loved only the stars
and not the sky which gave them space
in which to shine. Subtle, various,
sensitive, you are the skin of our terrain,
you're our democracy. When I understood
I had never honored you as a living
equal, I was ashamed of myself,
as if I had not recognised
a character who looked so different from me,
but now I can see us all, made of the
same basic materials –
cousins of that first exploding from nothing –
in our intricate equation together. O dirt,
help us find ways to serve your life,
you who have brought us forth, and fed us,
and who at the end will take us in
and rotate with us, and wobble, and orbit.

WOODWIND ODE

When the temperature drops, and the wind begins
to moan, through the coils of the air conditioner,
and I wonder how the wind chooses
its notes, yowling quietly
along a certain minor range,
suddenly I understand
that the passageways in the appliance are shaped
to make a D♭, which slides up to
E, F, F#, and back
down again, as the breeze freshens
and subsides. The conch has notes in it,
Silurian notes, and the horn of the ram,
the shofar, has notes – instruments
were made to resemble caves, with Aeolian
tunnels, through which the gods spoke,
and through the didgeridoo with its six-foot
mourning throat and its mouth of honeybee
wax, and through the brasses. And for how many eons
    had we
heard the big cats' sexual
howling before we took their guts and made
strings of them, how many eras had our
primate predecessors groaned, while
making the next generation,
before a homo sapiens
looked at another homo sapiens,
seeing her or his body as a
melody-producing shape, wondering what
notes he could get
out of it.
And parents who beat their children, how much

are they in it for the song – to hear, again,
the music that was made on them
back at the beginning, world with end, no amen.

NEW ENGLAND CAMPING ODE

We're driving through a state forest,
he says it would take a summer — from last
frost, to first frost — to walk
the Appalachian Trail. You would mail yourself
two-week packets of dried food
to a dozen small-town post offices . . .
And I think, for a minute, what it would be like
to wake at first light, and go to your little
hand-dug latrine — after some months,
the dirt-filled pits like the dotted line behind
Vasco da Gama's ship on the map — then add
sticks to the coals for the new day's fire, and boil
water for coffee, pack in a dozen
sugar cubes, for each day,
168 for two weeks,
box like a building made of rough bright rooms,
then strike camp, and walk among
the ancestors. For a moment, I imagine
that journey of a summer. And then I wonder, how
much of the fear which many women
have of dangerous men in the woods
do many men have of dangerous
men in the woods. Half? A quarter?
An eighth of a teaspoon? And how much of our fear is that
during the rape, we know that he is likely
to kill us when he's done. Forgive me, pines and
beeches, hemlocks and larches, forgive me
branches, leaves, needles, cones,
spiders' webs, lichens, nests,
dragonfly camping out
in the air, his food stored in it,
forgive me, damselfly, beating her

wings in the web, suddenly soaring
out, forgive me for speaking of such scenes
here in your home of forage and order
I may not, for my fearful nature,
enter, for a summer.

PINE TREE ODE

I was sitting on the top stones of a wall – can you
get even closer to the tree, he said, so I went
inches from the trunk of the tallest of the ones
we'd been standing among like small children
among the legs of the grown-ups.
Now, the side of my face was almost
against the bark, intimate,
I could see where its growing had pulled its surface
open, into wooden lozenges, like
stretch marks, I could not feel it breathe
but I felt it alive beside me, a huge
ant running down, and stopping, and turning
its feelers, in the air, between us, and then
walking so fast it seemed to be pouring
back up. Then I looked, up, along
the branchless stem, into the canopy,
to the needles fanning out in bunches
eating the sun. And the length of it seemed like
bravery, like strong will,
a single, whole, note, like a tenor's
cry, sustained, as if a tree were
a spurt from the earth, a heart's gush.
And the ants flowed from ground to sky,
sky to ground. I don't know where the ants
had been, or their ancestors had been, the noon
the tornado came through, wall of water
a hundred and thirty miles an hour,
solid ferocious grey static.
The tree stood. And now I sat up straight
beside it, feeling my way back
through species, and species, toward the pine, and toward

the ones we both descended from, the
fern, the green cell – the sun,
the star-stuff we are made of.

SLOAN KETTERING ODE

The hospital lobby was lined with short
and long views of Audubon's birds,
the tallest ones' necks curved, all the way
down, to fit into the life-size space
of the double octave. When I got upstairs
to my partner's brother's door, the curtain
was partly open, he was sitting up
on the raised bed, back in the corner
of the room, as if almost outside
the scene, at the edge of a clearing, his face
nearly empty of expression, except for
endurance and absence of hope. He was in pain
all the time now. His eyes were wide open,
like the eyes of someone shocked, but not
the emotion of shock, but the matter of it,
and, with his round glasses and upstretched
neck, he looked a little like a secretary bird,
backed up into a small enclosure.
And he was yellower than the last time,
an ocher color some warblers have on a
sunlit day, in shadow—for that moment,
before a look of recognition, or his
courteous smile, which could brighten so quickly into
warmth, he looked, to me, like some other kind of
being – elegant, alert, stunned –
and I realised I had walked into
his line of sight, and seen him looking at nothing.

TRILOBITE ODE

for Joshua Wallman

Last evening, a large spider perched
in the air, above and behind the head
of your younger, your surviving brother, my partner, then
the hunter ran down toward his hair, and took up
a fly and swift-wrapped it and ran back up into
the eave. And this morning, close above
the pond, a swallow sipped up a midsummer
insect. And here on the table is the silvery
shard of shale I chose from your things,
after you died, a smooth, heavy,
sedimentary rock-fragment
made by the earth when it was covered with vast,
warm, equatorial, shallow seas. At some
moment, this jointed one rested, here,
from its rippling swimming, its hunting, 500
million years ago, and died,
undulator as it had been.
And then our planet convulsed and froze, ex-
ploded thrust up, taking this scarab
Spartan to a mountaintop,
a meadow where a child at a picnic looked down,
and saw it, next to her own hand.
And in your photos, young, you looked
bemused, sometimes, your eyes lifted,
your mind at play. Sixty years later,
in your last days, as you lay in your small
home like some long-limbed ocher creature in a
dark and bright sea, this flattish marine
arthropod was lying in the room,
Elrathia kingii, 'having the body
divided,' below the big, shield

brow, 'by two furrows, into
three parts,' the flexible segments
making the lines of a musical score
for twelve tones. In the time you had,
you recorded every note you could,
you wrote out the music of a life, and left it
to us, here, where we replay it, and long for more, and replay it.

DOUBLE ODE FOR HAZEL

She carried rain into the house.
She shook herself, and in a circle around her
she rained. She carried in snow, in knobs,
in her comb-honey coat, knots which she heated
and melted. She dropped herself down by the stove,
domestic percussion of her bones on hardwood,
and steamed. And she carried her panting out of the
house, and it entered the local wind,
as mist – all this done not by her will,
but done by her, the earth's creature.
Sometimes she carried a chicken bone
out through the door, or waited on
the sill for it to be laid in the jaws
she knew to keep open, and wait. She carried –
she was – a devotion beyond my measuring,
which traveled, dawn to dusk, to dark, one
way and then another, over
the sill of her dwelling, where her beloved,
her ruler, commanded the clang of the metal
can which held her meals, and which, when it was
opened, rang like an aluminum gong.
And in the woods, she would chase food
which lived, she would dig and nose for it,
and when he said her name, she would,
reluctant, desist, and follow, ahead
or behind. Sometimes, when she needed to go out,
she would rear up, like a long-haired sun-colored
pony, at the door, and when it opened, last night,
she ran, head down, in a straight line
out into the cold spring evening, and did not
come back, when called, in the night or morning.

Now somewhere on her native ground
are her elements being returned to it,
her breath, her spirit, to the air we will breathe now,
looking for her, wand passed in and
out of the house – Hazel, light of the home.

2.

It wasn't like her, not to come back after
supper. He leaned out the door and called,
and the lack of those sounds of her beginning to run
to his voice – at first a few hairs of sound, like a
low breeze, plume of a tail
along a bush, paw on beech leaf –
was eerie, like an illusion. Later,
he went out, into the dark, and called.
Just that morning, he had showed me the picture
of her late mother, the English shepherd so
ferocious people laugh in wonder
when her name comes up – in the photo she was lying
regal, the black pups of her litter
sucking, the one amber one
not visible – probably under
the others, he said, he chose her because
she had the most intelligent,
submissive nature. Hazel!, he called
into the night. We sat by the fire,
reading, and the room wasn't itself,
and though I dismissed it, there came into my mind
a picture of her as I had never seen her,
lying down, near one of the trails – not
on the path of pressed cones and
leaves and moss, but on a rougher
bed of twigs and needles and lichen
and flecks of quartzite from granite, and in
the vision she did not stir, she who is the

soul of stirring – I dismissed it, but I had
seen it, as if she were beginning to return
into the earth. I don't know when he thought
to check the jeep – he had not taken her
out in it – but when he opened its door,
there she was, all curves of butter
coat, curvetting with joy to see him.
Trained, by him, not to bark
except at intruders,
she'd remained quiet, in the car, when we'd stood
just yards from her, calling her name.
As I ramped my hands in her loose, luxurious
pelt, it was as if I could feel
the sweet chance of her livingness,
as if her elements had begun
to be dispersed, and then flew back
together, to create this being
of devotion, his longest, his golden, companion.

HARMONY ODE

And when they stroke the curtain aside,
gilded-thread lions, on milk-color cloth,
and open the doors of the ark – the small,
brightly lit, room—there is not
an instrument of torture, inside,
but a book, or not a book, but a scroll,
for singing, three scrolls, in embroidered robes,
with sashes, with polished silver crowns.
And then, for the rest of the service – while we're hearing of
a Him, and a Him, and a He – I do what I've been
doing all my life, with singing, seeking,
above its shaded melodious woods of
baritone and bass, the harmony,
the descant, the higher the woman tones, which
lift your spirit, and burnish it,
above the deeper boles, trunks,
mosses, earth, stone. It is what I had
done as a child, in church, listened,
listened for my mother's soprano and then
gone with my voice to join it, in its seeking,
and finding, in its bliss-seeking resolve,
what goes with, and makes complete, from above,
and does not dominate, but smoothes,
strengthens. It was a fathers' world,
but with a mother's voice on it.
The world was their pool, in shadow, but with
our light on it.

What is greed? 'Excessive desire
for getting or having; desire for more than one
needs or deserves.' But if a granary
is full of grain, and the waterwheel
is turning, why not pour out every
golden room, in turn? You cannot
garner more than is there, nor are there
mice to gorge on what might remain
unswept from the corners, unwrung from the shimmering
husk-dust of the walls – the genome says,
Make more of me. You can hear *greed*
in Old English *graedum,* 'eagerly,'
and Gothic *gredags,* 'hunger,' and Indo-Euro-
pean **gher-,* 'to crave'. But the species
loves when a woman's knees ripple
like mirages, she can hardly walk, and any new
conceptus inside her has more time to cast its anchor,
and hunker, and double, and dodecadouble
itself. We are animals of multiplication, our
times-tables love to have themselves out
like orgasms, to the last decimal
out at the curve of matter where spirit free-
falls, into a nothing so full,
so arable, so satiable.

DONNER PARTY MOTHER ODE

I'm glad that my mother was cremated whole,
despite the operatic crackling and
Medean explosions in the box, and the singing
of the fat as it gave up its dazzling ghost,
glad she was consumed to ash,
and cooled, and dried – though some animal grease
remained, I felt it, I felt awe to touch it.
And I'm glad that – with prayers, with sobbing,
and awe – she was let go, by her children, like
grey down, onto the cold
bosomy swells of the bay, where she sank
in clouds of changing shape, in chalky
spirals, like a child dancing when no one
can see her. I am glad that my mother
was dispersed, I am glad she is everywhere
and nowhere. And could I have feasted on my mother,
at Donner Lake? I think she might have
wanted me to – there was, in her, when she was
old, such a new pleasure that I
was alive. And I think – maybe sitting in
her kitchen, we could have joked about it, *I
think I'd start with your earlobes,*
I might have said to her, as if flirting – and I can
see my mom saying, *you know where I'd
start with you Shar, your best part,*
my favorite part – how I fooled my mother –
your loving heart – how I've tried to fool
myself, as if all my life I have not loved her and mourned her.

ABRACADABRA ODE

```
A B R A C A D A B R A
A B R A C A D A B R
A B R A C A D A B
A B R A C A D A
A B R A C A D
A B R A C A
A B R A C
A B R A
A B R
A B
A
```

When we think about how women have fared, let's
remember the amulet carried in the ancient
world – on a tiny parchment, the written-out
word, *A B R A C A D A B R A,* then each
letter again underneath, one step
to the right: first, the slanted-in column
of *A*s; then *B*s, the next layer in;
and then the *R*s, and then more *A*s,
and the *C*s – each horizontal row stopping short one
space from the one above it, until there's
a triangle, a spell in a *V*
like a mound of Venus. Could it heal us? Could our prayers
be heard: *abracadabra,* from
the Aramaic, *abhadda ked-habra,*
'Disappear, O sickness, at the sound of this word.'

ACKNOWLEDGEMENTS

Acknowledgements are due to the editors of the following:

American Poetry Review, Cortland Review, Five Points, Freeman's, Green Mountain Review, Harvard Review, New Yorker, Ploughshares, poets.org, Prairie Schooner, Slate, Southern Review, Threepenny Review, Tin House, Tracking the Storm, TriQuarterly, Urban Land Ethic